THE ARABIAN HORSE

By Sara Green

Consultant:
Dr. Emily Leuthner
DVM, MS, DACVIM
Country View Veterinary Service
Oregon, Wisc.

BELLWETHER MEDIA • MINNEAPOLIS, MN

Jump into the cockpit and take flight with Pilot Books. Your journey will take you on high-energy adventures as you learn about all that is wild, weird, fascinating, and fun!

This edition first published in 2012 by Bellwether Media, Inc.

No part of this publication may be reproduced in whole or in part without written permission of the publisher. For information regarding permission, write to Bellwether Media, Inc., Attention: Permissions Department, 5357 Penn Avenue South, Minneapolis, MN 55419.

Library of Congress Cataloging-in-Publication Data

Green, Sara, 1964-
The Arabian horse / by Sara Green.
      p. cm. – (Pilot Books. Horse breed roundup)
Includes bibliographical references and index.
Summary: "Engaging images accompany information about the Arabian horse. The combination of high-interest subject matter and narrative text is intended for students in grades 3 through 7"–Provided by publisher.
ISBN 978-1-60014-656-5 (hardcover : alk. paper)
1. Arabian horse–Juvenile literature. I. Title.
SF293.A8G74 2012
636.1'12–dc22   2011014594

Printed in the United States of America, North Mankato, MN.
080111   1187

CONTENTS

The Arabian Horse

Whoosh! A streak of color flashes before you. A cloud of dust blocks your view. As the dust settles, a striking Arabian slows down in the distance. It rears up onto its hind legs and shakes its beautiful mane. Long ago, people gave Arabians the nickname "Drinkers of the Wind" for their speed. Today, people admire the intelligence, **endurance**, and friendly **temperament** of the breed. The Arabian is one of the most popular horses in the world.

Arabians are known for their beauty. They have small heads, pointed ears, and long, graceful necks. Their **muzzles** are narrow enough to fit into a teacup. A delicate **dish** dips between their large, wide-set eyes. Their long manes are silky, and their tails are carried high. The magnificent Arabian attracts attention wherever it goes!

A Rib Short

Some Arabians have one less rib than other horse breeds. They have 35 ribs instead of the usual 36.

Arabians are smaller than most horses. They weigh between 800 and 1,100 pounds (360 and 500 kilograms) and stand 14 to 15 **hands** high at the **withers**. One hand equals 4 inches (10.2 centimeters). That makes Arabians 56 to 60 inches (142 to 152 centimeters) tall.

Most **purebred** Arabians have coats in one of six colors. These are bay, chestnut, black, gray, roan, and white. Bay Arabians have reddish brown coats with black manes and tails. Chestnut Arabians are copper in color. Roan Arabians have black, chestnut, or bay coats mixed with white hairs. Many Arabians have white markings on their legs and faces. Most Arabians have black skin, except under their white marks. The dark skin protects them from sunburn.

chestnut
Arabian

Arabian Coat Colors

bay

roan

white

A Desert History

The Arabian is the oldest **domesticated** horse breed in the world. Arabians first appeared on the Arabian Peninsula over 4,500 years ago. Ancient Egyptian artwork shows these horses pulling chariots into battle. Later, the Bedouin people began using Arabians. The Bedouins are **nomads** who have lived in the deserts of the **Middle East** for at least 2,000 years. Their horses had to be fast and brave to run quickly in and out of battle. They needed endurance to travel long distances with little food or water in hot desert temperatures. The Bedouins chose the strongest, fastest Arabian horses to have **foals**. These foals are the **ancestors** of today's Arabians.

The Bedouins treated their Arabians very well. They shared food and water with them. They even let their horses sleep with them in their tents. In turn, the horses learned to trust the Bedouin people. They were kind and gentle with their riders.

Arabian Bloodlines

Over time, people crossed Arabians with other breeds. Arabian blood improved the speed, endurance, and strength of many horses. The Thoroughbred, American Saddlebred, and American Quarter Horse breeds all have Arabian ancestors.

In the 600s, the **Prophet** Muhammad and his followers worked to spread **Islam** throughout the Middle East. They used Arabians to travel. Leaders of countries across the region became aware of the strong, fast breed. They wanted Arabian horses of their own. From the late 1600s to the 1800s, people in the Middle East and Europe started large Arabian horse farms. During times of war, Arabians served as military horses. In times of peace, people rode Arabians for pleasure, traded them, and gave them as gifts.

An Arabian Legend

According to legend, Muhammad once locked up 100 Arabian mares and did not give them water for three days. When he finally freed them, they all ran toward a nearby pool of water. Muhammad then blew a horn, calling the horses to battle. Most of the horses ignored the horn and kept running. However, five mares stopped and returned to Muhammad. These five mares helped start the Arabian horse breed.

In 1893, a group of Turkish people brought 45 purebred Arabians to the World's Fair in Chicago. Americans loved the look of these graceful horses and began breeding them. The Arabian Horse Club of America formed in 1908 to record Arabians and their ancestors. The organization's name was later changed to the Arabian Horse Association (AHA). It **registers** any foal that has two purebred Arabian parents. Today, more than 600,000 Arabians are registered with the AHA.

Distance Racing and Dressage

Arabians are champions in long-distance riding events. These competitions test a horse's endurance and a rider's **horsemanship**. Some events require riders to travel 100 miles (161 kilometers) in one day. To win a long-distance ride, a horse and its rider must be in great physical shape and have a very strong bond.

Beginning riders travel on short, smooth trails. Advanced riders face trails that are longer and rougher. These trails often have obstacles such as creeks and fallen trees. Most long-distance riders do not focus on winning. They are happy just to cross the finish line. Riding a horse over a long trail is a remarkable achievement. If you want to see an Arabian at its best, attend a long-distance riding event!

Strength to Finish

Veterinarians examine horses at rest stops throughout long-distance rides. They make sure the horses are healthy enough to continue the race.

Arabians can compete in two kinds of long-distance rides. **Endurance rides** test for speed. The first horse to cross the finish line is the winner. One of the most famous endurance rides is the Tevis Cup. During this one-day, 100-mile (160-kilometer) ride, participants travel through the Sierra Nevada. The first Tevis Cup was held in 1955 and had only a few riders. Today, up to 250 people and their horses participate every year.

Competitive trail rides test the horse's physical fitness, the rider's horsemanship, and the team's pace. Veterinarians check the heart rates and breathing rates of horses before and after a competition. They give scores based on the changes in these rates. Horsemanship judges give scores on how well a rider handles his or her horse. Points are given before a ride for presentation and mounting. During the ride, riders are judged on how well they guide their horses across streams, over logs, and up and down hills. Finally, riders are given a score on how well they pace their horses throughout the competition. The horse and rider team with the fewest physical changes, best horsemanship, and best pace wins!

The intelligent, athletic Arabian also excels in **dressage**. Beginning skills in dressage include precisely controlled **gaits** and turns. More advanced movements are piaffes and pirouettes. A piaffe is a move in which a horse stands in place and performs a **trot**. For a pirouette, a horse turns in a tight circle at a **canter**. Some horses even perform **choreographed** movements set to music. It takes years of practice and hard work to learn these advanced movements.

In dressage competitions, horses and riders show their skills in front of judges and an audience. Judges give scores to each horse and its rider. Top scoring teams win bronze, silver, or gold medals. With their graceful style, many Arabians have won medals in the dressage arena.

All Dressed Up

In dressage competitions, riders wear coats, tall boots, and hats. It is a tradition for riders to braid their horses' manes.

Famous Arabians

Marengo

Marengo was a small, gray Arabian stallion that belonged to Napoleon I of France during the late 1700s and early 1800s. Marengo is remembered for his bravery and endurance in war. Although he was wounded eight times, Marengo carried Napoleon in all his battles. He was captured at the Battle of Waterloo and taken to England. There, he fathered many foals. Marengo died at the age of 38 in 1831. Today, his skeleton is on display at the National Army Museum in London, England.

Cass Ole

Cass Ole was a black Arabian stallion from Texas. He won over 50 show horse championships. He was also famous for his role as "The Black" in the movies *The Black Stallion* and *The Black Stallion Returns*. He had a special black wig woven into his mane to make his hair look longer in the movies. He also visited the White House and was present at the inauguration of U.S. President Ronald Reagan. After retiring from public life, he lived on a Texas ranch, where he fathered over 130 foals.

Arabians have been working and living with people for thousands of years. Their beauty, grace, endurance, and intelligence have made them one of the most popular horse breeds in the world. Today's purebred Arabians have the same qualities as those ridden long ago by the Bedouins in the Middle East. People continue to appreciate the speed and strength that made Arabians dependable desert horses. Now they are known as long-distance trail riding champions and fun family horses. Whether you're new to riding or an expert on horseback, Arabian horses are sure to win your heart!

Glossary

ancestors—family members who lived long ago

canter—a controlled gait that is faster than a trot but slower than a gallop

choreographed—having a planned sequence of steps and moves

dish—the inward slope below the eyes of a horse

domesticated—tamed; domesticated animals are used to living near people.

dressage—a specific kind of horse training; dressage horses perform movements like spins and turns at the command of their riders.

endurance—the ability to do something for a long time

foals—young horses; foals are under one year old.

gaits—the ways in which a horse moves; walking, trotting, and cantering are examples of gaits.

hands—the units used to measure the height of a horse; one hand is equal to 4 inches (10.2 centimeters).

horsemanship—the riding, training, and handling of horses

Islam—a religion that follows the teachings of the Prophet Muhammad; followers of Islam are called Muslims.

Middle East—an area of southwest Asia and northeast Africa that stretches from the Mediterranean Sea to Pakistan

muzzles—the mouths and noses of some animals

nomads—people who have no specific home and travel from place to place

prophet—a person said to speak for a god

purebred—born from parents of the same breed

registers—makes record of; owners register their horses with official breed organizations.

temperament—personality or nature; the Arabian has a friendly temperament.

trot—a controlled gait that is faster than a walk but slower than a canter

withers—the ridge between the shoulder blades of a horse

To Learn More

At the Library

Braulick, Carrie A. *The Arabian Horse*. Mankato, Minn.: Capstone Press, 2005.

Rumsch, BreAnn. *Arabian Horses*. Edina, Minn.: ABDO Pub., 2011.

Stone, Lynn M. *Arabian Horses*. Vero Beach, Fla.: Rourke Pub., 2008.

On the Web

Learning more about Arabian horses is as easy as 1, 2, 3.

1. Go to www.factsurfer.com.

2. Enter "Arabian horses" into the search box.

3. Click the "Surf" button and you will see a list of related Web sites.

With factsurfer.com, finding more information is just a click away.

Index

The images in this book are reproduced through the courtesy of: Juniors Bildarchiv / Age Fotostock, front cover; Mark J. Barrett / KimballStock, pp. 4-5; Ron Kimball / KimballStock, p. 7 (top); Ellwood Eppard, p. 7 (left, middle, & right); DEA / G. DAGLI ORTI / Getty Images, p. 8 (small); BIOS / Photolibrary, pp. 8-9; Klein-Hubert / KimballStock, p. 11; James Puttick, pp. 12-13; Lynne Glazer, pp. 14-15; Dennis Donohue, pp. 16-17; Karen Givens, pp. 18-19; PICANI PICANI / Photolibrary, pp. 20-21.